FINDING YOUR VOICE

*An Empowering Journey for Women
to Worthiness, Confidence & Self-Love*

ANN C.K. NICKELL

100th Man
Publishing

Finding Your Voice
by Ann C.K. Nickell

© 2025 by Ann C.K. Nickell

Published by
100th Man Publishing
www.100thmanpublishing.com

Printed in the United States of America.

All rights reserved. This book or parts thereof may not be reproduced in any form, stored in any retrieval system, or transmitted in any form by any means – electronic, mechanical, photocopy, recording, or otherwise – without prior written permission of the publisher. The only exception is brief quotations in printed reviews.

To every woman who has made it this far.

The one who kept going even when it was hard.

The one who is still standing after life tried to silence her.

You are worthy of your voice.

You are worthy of purpose and joy.

You are worthy of a life that feels true to who you are.

It is not too late. You are not behind. You are becoming.

You deserve a beautiful life.

WELCOME TO YOUR JOURNEY OF BECOMING

You are here because something inside you is ready for more. More peace. More truth. More you.

Maybe you've spent years quieting your voice to keep the peace, putting others first, and you lost sight of your own needs. Maybe you've been told you're too sensitive, too emotional, too much. Or maybe you've simply forgotten how powerful and worthy you are. I understand, because I've been there.

When I was young, people often told me I had a voice. They called me brave. Smart. Self-reliant. Confident. But after years of bullying, stress, and anxiety, I lost that confidence. I buried my voice deep inside, afraid to let it out. I let others dictate my life and write my story. But hiding it away didn't make life easier. It made it harder. I sank deeper into despair until, after 20 years in an emotionally abusive marriage, I finally reached a breaking point. I finally gained the courage I needed to leave.

It wasn't easy or glamorous. It was messy, scary, and lonely. But it was the moment I stopped waiting for someone else to save me. I chose freedom over security. I chose my voice over silence. And everything began to change. Today, I have a new life and purpose.

I want to help you find your voice, too, and discover the freedom and peace that comes with it. This book is your invitation to come home to yourself.

Finding Your Voice: An Empowering Journey for Women to Worthiness, Confidence & Self-Love is more than a book. It's a mirror, a safe place, and a guide back to the truth:

You matter. Your voice matters. Your story matters.

Through these ten steps, you'll gently peel back the layers of shame, fear, and self-doubt that have kept you small. You'll learn to listen to your inner voice, speak your truth with compassion, and stand firmly in your worth. You'll reclaim your space in the world, not with force, but with quiet strength and grounded confidence.

Each step is designed to nurture you, not rush you. There's no "perfect" way to move through this. Go at your own pace. Pause when you need. Celebrate the small shifts. This is your journey, and you get to decide how it unfolds.

You are not broken. You don't need fixing.

You are healing. You are remembering. You are rising.

So take a deep breath. Open your heart. And let's begin.

With love,

Ann C.K. Nickell
The Story Shepherd

ROADMAP OF THE BOOK

STEP ONE:

CREATE A SAFE, SUPPORTIVE SPACE

STEP TWO:

IDENTIFY YOUR INNER NARRATIVE

STEP THREE:

PRACTICE SELF-LOVE AND WORTHINESS

STEP FOUR:

CLARIFY YOUR NEEDS AND DESIRES

STEP FIVE:

SET MINI BOUNDARIES

ROADMAP OF THE BOOK

STEP SIX:

REDEFINE ASSERTIVENESS AS LOVE

STEP SEVEN:

HEAL THE ROOT WOUNDS

STEP EIGHT:

CELEBRATE PROGRESS AND SMALL WINS

STEP NINE:

TAKE OWNERSHIP OF YOUR LIFE

STEP TEN:

REWRITE YOUR SELF-STORY

Safety is the soil where healing takes root.

STEP ONE

Create a Safe, Supportive Space

Purpose: Build trust within yourself so you feel seen, heard, and not judged.

Before any transformation can happen, you need to feel emotionally safe. Start by creating a calm, comforting environment. Try lighting a candle, playing soft music, or wrapping yourself in a cozy blanket.

Let your space signal to your nervous system: "I am safe here."

Then create emotional safety by practicing self-kindness.

Let go of self-judgment. Let yourself feel what you feel, without trying to fix or change it right away.

I am safe. My voice matters.
I am seen. I speak my truth with clarity and courage.
I am supported. I am worthy of love and kindness.

Breathe in safety. Breathe out fear.

Repeat this daily.

Creating Safe Spaces

Creating a safe space, physically, emotionally, mentally, and spiritually, is a powerful first step in a healing journey.

For women, especially those reclaiming their voice and sense of worth, this can mean both setting up a comforting external environment and cultivating internal safety.

For me, emotional safety didn't begin with bubble baths or soft music. It began the night I broke. When the weight of years in an emotionally abusive marriage became too heavy, and I lost myself in the darkness.

That low moment wasn't the end. It was the beginning. I didn't know how I was going to leave. I just knew I had to go. So I started creating space where I could breathe again.

In the quiet moments when he was gone, I prayed. I read books that reminded me I wasn't crazy, that gaslighting was real, and that healing was possible. I lit candles. I wrapped myself in my favorite blanket. I took walks by the lake and fed the ducks. I surrounded myself with images of peace, of beaches, lighthouses, and still water.

I didn't feel strong yet. But in those moments, I started whispering to myself:

"You are safe here."
"You are allowed to dream again."
"You matter."

This is what creating a safe space looks like when you've been told your needs don't matter. It's not about the perfect room. It's about creating moments of peace in the chaos. It's about building emotional safety one breath, one prayer, and one quiet act of self-kindness at a time.

Before any transformation can happen, you need to feel emotionally safe. Let your space, even if it's just a chair by a window or a few quiet minutes alone, send a signal to your nervous system:

"I am safe here. I am allowed to feel. I am allowed to begin again."

Here are some meaningful ways a woman can create a safe space:

Physical Safe Space Ideas

These help calm the body and signal to the nervous system that it's okay to relax:

- Design a cozy corner: Fill it with soft blankets, pillows, a journal, candles, and comforting items.
- Use sensory comfort tools: Soft lighting, essential oils (lavender, chamomile), herbal tea, calming textures, or a weighted blanket.
- Play soothing sounds: Nature sounds, calming instrumental music, or ambient noise apps.
- Create a visual sanctuary: Add affirmations, calming artwork, or photos that make you feel loved and empowered.

Emotional Safe Space Practices

This is about how you treat yourself inside your mind and heart:

- Practice self-compassion: Speak to yourself like a best friend. Say, "It's okay to feel this," or "I'm doing the best I can."
- Validate your emotions: Allow yourself to feel without minimizing or rushing to "fix" things.
- Set gentle boundaries: Say no to energy-draining people or tasks. Give yourself permission to protect your peace.
- Limit negative input: Take breaks from news, toxic social media, or environments that make you feel small.
- Journal regularly: Let your thoughts and feelings have a home. It creates emotional release and clarity.

Mental Safe Space Habits

Create a mindset that nurtures growth and healing.

- Use positive self-talk: Replace criticism with encouragement. "I'm learning." "I'm healing". "I'm allowed to take up space."
- Practice mindfulness: Ground yourself with breathwork or body scans when feeling overwhelmed.
- Create daily rituals: Morning tea with affirmations, bedtime gratitude journaling, or midday breathwork breaks.
- Avoid perfectionism: Embrace progress over perfection. Celebrate small wins.

Religious or Spiritual Safe Space Rituals

Create a space that also nurtures your soul.

- Prayer: Connect with God to feel held and guided.
- Meditation: Connect with the world to find peace.
- Affirmations or mantras: Repeat grounding phrases like: "I am worthy." "I am enough." "I am safe now."
- Sacred objects: Keep crosses or other faith symbols, crystals, or meaningful keepsakes in your space.

Creating a safe, supportive space is not just about external comfort. It's an act of self-honoring. It tells your mind, body, and spirit: I am worthy of gentleness. I am allowed to feel. I belong here.

Whether it's through soft lighting, comforting words, or simply pausing to breathe, each small choice to care for yourself lays the foundation for deeper healing.

Creating a safe, supportive space is not a luxury. It is the foundation for every chapter that follows.

Before you can find your voice, challenge old beliefs, or dream again, your nervous system must know that it is no longer under threat. Safety allows truth to surface. Gentleness makes healing possible.

Each small act of self care is a quiet declaration that you are worthy of protection and peace.

This is where your healing story begins, not with force or fixing, but with compassion.

As you continue this journey, return to this space often. Let it be the place where you are seen, heard, and welcomed back to yourself, again and again.

Journal Prompt: What helps me feel emotionally and physically safe?

Creating a Safe, Supportive Space

Personal Notes / Journaling

Creating a Safe, Supportive Space

Personal Notes / Journaling

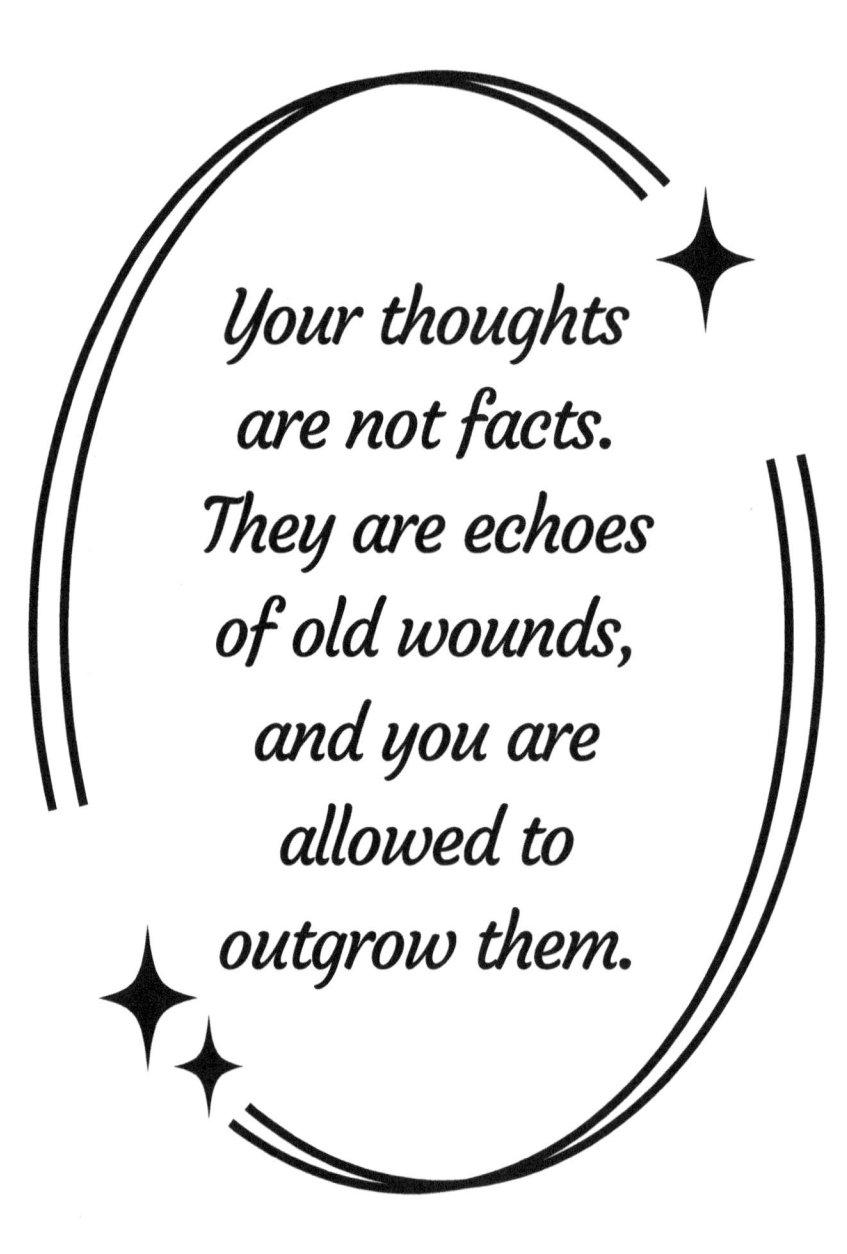

Identify Your Inner Narrative

Purpose: Uncover the core beliefs that are holding you back.

Notice the stories you've been telling yourself. Maybe it's, "I don't matter". Or maybe, "If I speak up, I'll be rejected".

These thoughts are not facts. They're old beliefs, often rooted in fear or past wounds.

Begin to name your thoughts.

Ask yourself: Is this belief coming from fear or love? Is it still true?

These thoughts are not who I am.
I choose truth over fear.

Sit quietly and picture each limiting belief floating away like a cloud.

Repeat this daily.

Uncover Core Beliefs that are Holding You Back

Uncovering the core beliefs that are holding you back is a courageous and transformative act. It allows you to see the roots of your self-doubt, fear, and silence.

For years, the story I carried sounded like this:

"You're too emotional."
"You're too sensitive."
"You're not good enough."
"People don't like the real you."

These weren't just passing thoughts. They became my inner script, whispered to me through years of bullying, anxiety, and emotional abuse. They clung to me like a second skin, shaping how I saw myself.

Eventually, I married a man who mirrored those lies. For over 20 years, I lived under the weight of a controlling, emotionally abusive marriage that chipped away at my voice and my confidence, one silent compromise at a time. I gave up my dreams, my independence, even my family, all while pretending things were "fine." But deep down, I believed I wasn't allowed to want more. That I had to stay small to stay safe.

Then one night, after an especially painful fight, I subconsciously hurt myself. I hit a breaking point and finally saw the truth. That the voice inside me saying "I don't want this life" wasn't wrong. It was my true self, begging to be heard.

That breaking point gave me the courage to finally leave, and I began to peel back the layers of fear and conditioning. I realized those voices weren't mine. They came from people who didn't see my worth and didn't know how to honor my heart. But somewhere along the way, I mistook their judgment for truth.

Acknowledging those inner narratives was the beginning of releasing them.

Later, when I nearly died after a medical crisis, those old stories came back louder than ever:

"You're broken now."
"You should give up."

But I refused to believe those stories. I talked back to them. I claimed a new narrative:

"I am resilient. I am called. I am a warrior. I am a walking miracle."

And that voice, the one that spoke with faith, grit, and truth, became louder than the lies.

You have that voice too. It might feel faint right now, but it's there, waiting for you to listen.

While noticing your inner stories is a powerful first step, there are several other techniques and reflective tools that can help you dig deeper into those hidden, limiting beliefs.

Pay Attention to Emotional Triggers

- Notice situations that cause a strong emotional reaction (shame, anger, anxiety, guilt).
- Ask: What belief is underneath this reaction? (Example: Feeling jealous → Belief: "I'm not good enough."

Mirror Work

- Look into your eyes in a mirror and say things like, "I am worthy" or "I am allowed to speak up".
- Notice what feelings or resistance come up. That resistance often points to a hidden belief.

Listen to the "Shoulds"

- I should be quiet.
- I should always say yes.

These statements often reveal beliefs around value, worth, and roles.

Challenge them by asking: Who taught me this? Is it true?

Track Repeating Patterns

- Look at your relationships, career, self-care, and choices.
- What themes or blocks repeat? (Example: Always over-giving → Belief: "My value comes from what I do for others.")

Explore Childhood Messages

- Reflect on what you were taught (directly or indirectly) as a child:
    - What did you learn about your worth, voice, emotions, or needs?
    - Who were you trying to please, impress, or not upset?

Use the "5 Whys" Technique

- Choose a negative thought like: "I'm not confident enough to speak up."
- Ask "Why?" five times to dig down into the core belief.
    - Why? → I'm afraid people won't like what I say.
    - Why? → I think they'll judge me.
    - Why? → I believe I have to be perfect to be accepted.
- (Example core belief: "If I'm not perfect, I'm not lovable.")

Practice Stillness and Ask Empowering Reflection Questions

- "What do I believe about myself that keeps me small?"
- "What would I have to stop believing to feel free?"
- "Why am I afraid to show up fully as myself?"

Let your subconscious speak without overthinking. The answers may rise as feelings, words, or images.

Becoming aware of your inner narrative is not about judging yourself or reliving old pain. It's about finally telling the truth with compassion.

The beliefs you've uncovered were formed to protect you at one time, but they do not get to define your future. When you name the stories that keep you small, you loosen their grip and reclaim your authority as the author of your life.

Awareness is the beginning of freedom. As you continue this journey, remember: you are not broken, behind, or too late. You are awakening.

And now that you can hear and understand the old story, you are ready to choose a new one. A story rooted in truth, courage, and the quiet knowing that your voice has always mattered.

Journal Prompt: What are the critical or fearful things you often say to yourself? What can you say instead?

Identify Your Inner Narrative

Personal Notes / Journaling

Identify Your Inner Narrative

Personal Notes / Journaling

Practice Self-Love and Worthiness

Purpose: Replace shame and unworthiness with kindness.

You are already worthy. You don't need to prove or earn it.

Begin treating yourself with the same compassion you offer to others. Speak kindly to yourself. Let yourself rest without guilt.

Create a daily self-kindness ritual.

Place your hand on your heart, say a kind word, or pause to breathe deeply.

> I am worthy of love.
> I give myself grace.
> I am enough.

Place your hand on your heart when you whisper this mantra to yourself.

Repeat this daily.

Self Kindness and Compassion Practices

Self-compassion is the foundation of worthiness.

When women begin treating themselves with the same care they offer others, transformation happens.

After I left my marriage, I thought freedom would feel easy. But instead of lightness, I felt grief, guilt, and a strange kind of silence. I kept thinking:

"Why did I wait so long?"
"How could I let it get that bad?"
"Why wasn't I stronger?"

I judged myself for staying, for not speaking up sooner, and for all the ways I had lost myself.

I prayed and asked for guidance, and one quiet morning, I placed my hand on my heart, closed my eyes, and whispered,
"You did the best you could. You were trying to survive."

That moment didn't erase the pain, but it changed my relationship to it. For the first time, I wasn't piling shame on top of wounds. I was tending to them.

Self-compassion became a daily practice. It meant noticing my inner critic, the voice that said I had to hustle to prove my worth, and choosing a kinder response.

It meant letting myself rest without guilt. It meant saying, "I matter too." It meant realizing that worth isn't something I had to earn, It was something I'd always had, buried under layers of fear and doubt.

And when I faced my medical crisis, that compassion became essential. On days when it hurt to walk, when healing felt slow, when I questioned everything, I gave myself grace. I looked at myself in the mirror and whispered again:

"You are strong. You are healing. You can do anything."

Learning to love myself as I was, not as I "should" be, changed everything.

That's what I want for you, too.

Here are ways to practice that compassion inwardly and gentle daily self kindness rituals you can incorporate into your healing journey.

Speak to Yourself Like a Best Friend

- Ask: What would I say to a friend going through this?
  - Then offer that same comfort to yourself without judgment or pressure to "fix" things.
- Ask, "What Do I Need Right Now?"
  - Then respond with a loving act: rest, space, food, or movement.

Celebrate Your Effort, Not Just Outcomes

- Notice and affirm your trying, your courage, your showing up, even if it wasn't perfect.

Forgive Yourself for Being Human

- Mistakes, emotional days, and missed goals are part of being human. Meet them with grace instead of shame. Say: "It's okay. I'm still learning."

Acknowledge Your Pain with Kindness

- When you're struggling, whisper inwardly: "This is hard, and I'm here for me."

Let Go of Harsh Inner Deadlines

- Give yourself permission to take the time you need, without guilt.

Protect Your Energy Like You'd Protect a Loved One

- Set boundaries. Say no. Step back from what drains you. This is love in action.

Love Note to Yourself

- Write a short note of encouragement and tuck it into your journal, purse, or mirror:
    - "I see how hard you're trying."
    - "You are worthy of peace."

Mirror Affirmation Moment

- Look yourself in the eyes in the mirror. Say something kind, like:
    - "You're doing beautifully."
    - "You're strong and a survivor."
    - "I love who you're becoming."

Gentle Wake-Up Ritual

- Instead of grabbing your phone first thing, place one hand on your belly, and one on your heart. Breathe and whisper:
    - "I'm allowed to go slowly. Today, I will be kind to me."
    - "I am worthy. I am safe. I am loved."

Nightly Kindness Reflection

- Before bed, write down in your journal:
    - One kind thing I did for myself.
    - One small win or strength I showed today.
    - One thing for which I forgive myself.

Practicing self-love is not about getting it right every day. It's about choosing kindness, again and again, especially on the days when it feels hardest.

Each gentle word you speak to yourself, each moment you allow rest without guilt, helps soften old wounds and release shame that was never yours to carry.

Worthiness is not something you earn through effort or perfection. It is something you remember by treating yourself with compassion.

As you continue this journey, let self-kindness be your guide.

Meet yourself where you are. Go slowly. Be gentle.

You are worthy of love, rest, and care, exactly as you are.

Journal Prompt: Reflect on a moment you were hard on yourself. Rewrite it with compassion.

Practice Self-Love and Worthiness

Personal Notes / Journaling

Practice Self-Love and Worthiness

Personal Notes / Journaling

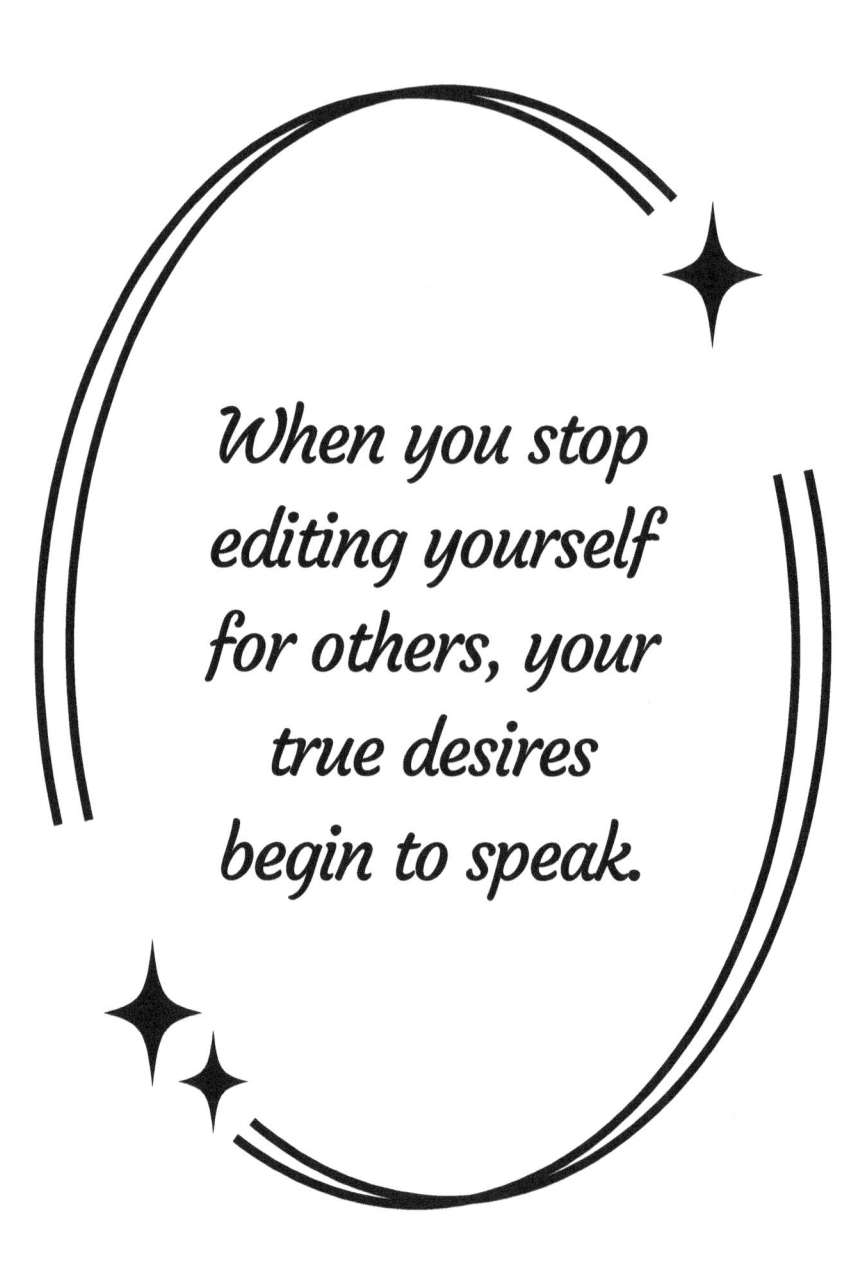

STEP FOUR

Clarify Your Needs and Desires

Purpose: Reconnect with what you truly want.

You may have spent years adapting to others, losing touch with what you really want.

Start paying attention to what brings you joy and what drains you.

Your needs and desires are important. They are the roadmap back to yourself.

MANTRA

My desires are valid.
My needs matter.

Visualize your heart gently opening and showing you what it longs for most.

Repeat this daily.

Reconnect with Your Own Needs and Desires

The practices in this step invite you to finally come home to yourself.

You may have spent years putting others first, dismissing your own needs as "too much" or "not important."

I spent decades deferring to everyone else; what they wanted, what they approved of, what made them comfortable. I followed the career path he encouraged. Drove the car he picked. Lived where he wanted. I was so used to adjusting myself to others that when someone finally asked me, "What do you want?", I froze. I didn't know how to answer.

At first, I felt ashamed for not knowing. Then I felt afraid of knowing. Because what if what I wanted didn't match what others expected of me? What if my desires made me look selfish or foolish?

It felt rebellious to admit I wanted to pursue my dreams. Dreams like publishing my books. Starting my own business. Driving a car that made me smile instead of shrink. Having a home where I could breathe and laugh and rest, not walk on eggshells.

But the more I listened, the clearer those longings became. Quiet at first, like whispers in a crowded room. Then louder, more persistent. Like my soul saying, "I'm still here. Please don't forget me."

Claiming those desires felt like breaking a sacred rule I was told never to break. But with each "yes" to myself, I uncovered a new part of who I really was. A woman with dreams. With passion. With vision. With a voice.

Now, every day, I ask myself:

What do I want? What do I need? What would feel good today?

And I let that voice lead.

Reconnecting with your true self means listening deeply, honoring your energy, and allowing yourself to want what you want.

Daily Check-In: "What Do I Need Right Now?

- Set a gentle reminder 1–2 times a day to pause and ask:
    - What does my body need?
    - What does my heart need?
    - What does my spirit need?
- Write the answer down, even if it's small (quiet, movement, laughter, reassurance).

Joy/Drain Inventory

- For 3–5 days, track:
    - What gave you energy, joy, peace?
    - What drained, frustrated, or overwhelmed you?
- At the end, look for patterns. This is data about your values and your needs.

Body Compass Exercise

- Think of a time you felt fully alive and joyful.
    - Where did you feel it in your body?
- Then recall a time you felt drained or stuck.
    - What did your body do (tense, tired, heavy)?
- Your body is a compass. Learn to listen to how it reacts to situations.

Create a "Yes & No" List

- Yes List: Things that feel good, energizing, aligned.
- No List: Things that feel draining, resentful, depleting.

Helps you begin setting boundaries and saying yes to more of what you truly want.

Inner Child Journaling

- Ask your younger self:
  - What did you love to do? What made you happy? What did you dream about?
- Often your truest desires have been with you since childhood.

Desire Mapping

- Ask:
  - How do I want to feel? (free, joyful, secure, seen)
  - What experiences, relationships, or environments support that feeling?
- This moves you from "goals" to soul-aligned desires.

Creative Expression

- Paint, collage, or create a vision board based on what brings you joy, not what's practical.
- The images that call to you often reflect your buried longings.

Create a Desire or Dream Journal

- Keep a notebook just for things you long for (big and small).
  - "I want more mornings to myself."
  - "I want to write a book."
  - "I want to feel light and free."
- Let it be a sacred space to listen to your heart without judgment.

Reconnecting with your true needs and desires is a quiet but radical act of self-honoring.

Each time you pause to ask, "What do I want? What do I need?" you are listening to the part of you that has been waiting to be heard. These desires are not selfish. They are the compass guiding you back to yourself.

Some answers will come easily. Others may take time, courage, and patience. Trust the process. Celebrate each small "yes" to yourself. Notice what brings you joy, what energizes you, and what drains you. Let these insights shape the choices you make, the boundaries you set, and the life you create.

By clarifying your needs and desires, you are giving yourself permission to step fully into your story, to claim your voice, and to live a life aligned with your heart.

This is the road back to you, and every step you take along it matters.

Journal Prompt: What would you choose today if no one else influenced your decision?

Clarify Your Needs and Desires

Personal Notes / Journaling

Clarify Your Needs and Desires

Personal Notes / Journaling

Set Mini-Boundaries

Purpose: Practice speaking up in low-stakes ways.

Start small. Practice saying what you want or don't want in gentle, clear ways.

Celebrate your effort, even if it feels awkward.

Boundaries are not selfish. They're an act of self-respect.

It is safe for me to say no.
I honor my energy.

Breathe deeply and imagine your boundaries as a warm, protective light.

Repeat this daily.

Developing Boundaries

Setting boundaries is one of the greatest acts of self-love and healing.

Many women have been conditioned to prioritize others' comfort over their own needs.

At first, even the smallest boundaries felt terrifying to me. I'd spent so many years putting other people's needs above my own that saying "no" felt like a threat; like I was risking love, safety, or approval. Somewhere along the way, I had absorbed the belief that being easygoing, agreeable, and accommodating made me "good."

But deep down, I was exhausted. I was resentful. I was disappearing.

When I started learning about boundaries, I thought they had to be loud or harsh to count. But I quickly discovered that even a quiet boundary is a powerful declaration of self-respect.

I started small, with:

"No, I don't want to watch that movie."
"I'm not available today."
"I'm spending a few hours alone to write."

And something unexpected happened: I didn't crumble. The world didn't fall apart. In fact, with every mini-boundary I set, I felt more rooted in myself. More honest. More whole.

Were there people who didn't like the change? Yes. But I realized that anyone who required me to shrink in order to stay wasn't really for me.

Setting boundaries helped me rebuild the foundation of my life. It reminded me that my energy is sacred, my time is valuable, and my voice deserves to be heard, even when it says no.

And now I'm reminding you:

You don't have to be loud to be clear. You don't have to be perfect to protect your peace. Every boundary you set is an act of self-love.

Learning to set boundaries, even in small ways, helps rebuild self-trust, confidence, and emotional safety.

Start with Self-Awareness

- Ask yourself regularly:
    - What feels okay to me, and what doesn't?
    - Where am I feeling drained, resentful, or overwhelmed?
- These feelings are signs that a boundary is needed.

Name One Boundary You Wish You Had

- Complete the sentence:
    - I wish I could say no to…
    - I wish I had more space around…
    - I wish others would stop…
- Then brainstorm what a small version of that boundary might look like.

Visualize Your Boundaries

- Imagine a protective circle or light around you.
- Picture yourself confidently communicating a boundary, calmly and clearly, and being respected.

Use the "Pause Before Yes" Practice

- When someone asks something of you, try saying:
    - "Let me check my schedule and get back to you."
    - "I'll need a moment to think about that."
- This gives you space to respond with intention, not guilt.

Use "I" Statements to Reduce Guilt

- Speak from your own experience rather than blaming:
    - "I need some space this weekend."
    - "I feel overwhelmed and need to step back."

Notice & Release Guilt

- Boundaries often bring up guilt at first.
- Journal:
    - What guilt am I feeling?
    - Where does that come from?
    - What would I say to a friend who felt this way?

Track Boundary Wins

- Each time you set a boundary, no matter how small, write it down.
- Celebrate it! "I said no to that meeting. I chose myself."
- This builds confidence over time.

Gentle Wake-Up Ritual

- Instead of grabbing your phone first thing, place one hand on your belly, one on your heart. Breathe and whisper:
    - "I'm allowed to go slowly. Today, I will be kind to me.
    - "I am worthy. I am safe. I am loved."

Affirm Your Right to Set Boundaries

- Repeat affirmations like:
    - "My needs matter."
    - "I am allowed to protect my peace."
    - "Boundaries create space for love, not distance."

Setting mini-boundaries is a quiet but powerful way to reclaim your time, energy, and voice.

Each small "yes" to yourself, and each gentle "no" to what drains you, is an act of self-respect and love.

Boundaries are not about being harsh or unkind. They are about honoring your needs and showing up as your truest self.

Remember, you don't need to set every boundary at once. Start small, notice your courage, and celebrate your wins. With each boundary you practice, you rebuild trust in yourself, strengthen your confidence, and create space for what truly matters.

Every step toward protecting your peace is a step toward a life where you are seen, valued, and free to thrive.

Journal Prompt: List five areas of your life where you'd like stronger boundaries (work, time, family, phone, emotions).

Set Mini-Boundaries

Personal Notes / Journaling

Set Mini-Boundaries

Personal Notes / Journaling

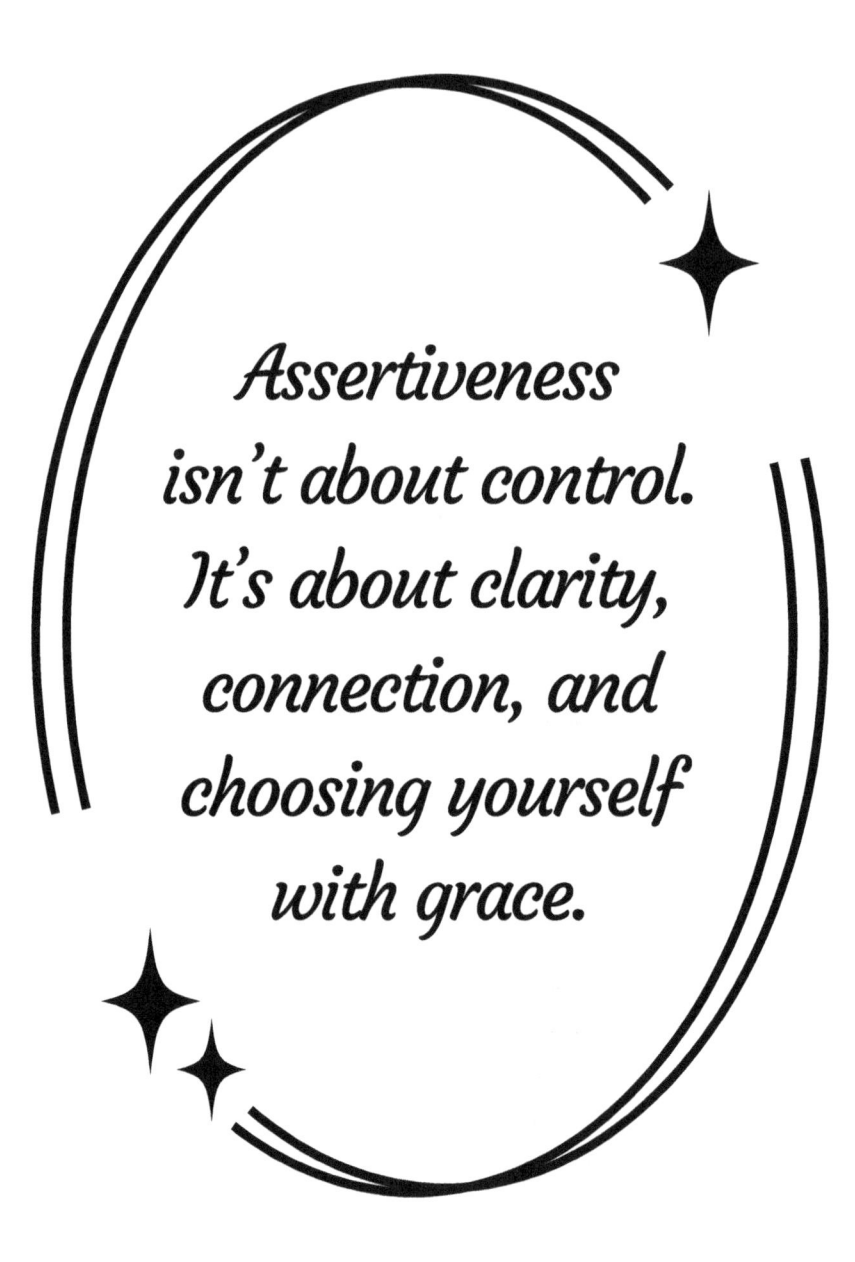

STEP SIX

Redefine Assertiveness as Love

Purpose: See speaking up as kind, not cruel.

You don't have to choose between being kind and being honest.

You can speak your truth with love.

Assertiveness is simply honoring your truth and needs, while still respecting others.

My voice is love.
Speaking up is a sacred act.

Picture yourself expressing your truth calmly and confidently.

Repeat this daily.

Speak Your Truth With Love

Redefining assertiveness as an act of love can be life-changing for women who've been taught that speaking up = conflict, rejection, or guilt.

This step is about healing the narrative that honesty is unkind and learning to see self-expression as a bridge, not a barrier.

I used to believe that being assertive was mean. That if I said how I really felt, or voiced a need, it would hurt someone, push them away, or make me "too much."

So I stayed quiet. I tiptoed. I twisted myself into whatever version of me made others comfortable. And honestly? I was scared. I thought love meant keeping the peace, even if it meant losing pieces of myself.

But after escaping an emotionally abusive marriage and then nearly losing my life and my leg, everything shifted. Those experiences cracked me wide open and showed me what really matters. And I realized something I'll never forget:

Love without truth isn't really love at all. Honesty is love. It's love for myself; my peace, my body, my voice. And it's love for the people around me, because they deserve my truth, not my silence.

I started practicing small phrases that felt gentle but clear:

"This doesn't work for me."
"Here's what I need right now."

At first, it felt awkward and unfamiliar, like trying a new language. But over time, I noticed how empowered I felt when I spoke up. How much safer I felt inside my own body. And how deeply people responded when I told the truth with kindness.

Now, I see assertiveness not as conflict, but as clarity. Not as selfish, but sacred. Because every time I speak up with love, I make space for real connection.

Here are some powerful practices and mindset shifts to help you speak your truth with love, grow in assertiveness, and feel safe being honest.

Shift the Narrative: Assertiveness = Connection, Not Conflict

- Journal or affirm:
    - "When I speak up, I invite real connection."
    - "Honesty is not cruelty, it's clarity."
    - "My truth doesn't need to hurt someone else's."

Start with Low-Stakes Honesty

- Practice being direct in simple, daily ways:
    - "I'd prefer the other restaurant."
    - "Actually, I don't enjoy that show. Can we pick something else?"
- Build up comfort gradually.

Write Your Truth First

- If speaking up feels scary, write what you want to say first.
- This can help you gain clarity and soften your delivery with intention and care.

Ask Yourself: What Would I Tell a Friend?

- If a friend were in your situation, what would you encourage her to say or do?
- Then give yourself that same permission.

Nurture Your Inner Voice

- Speak to yourself like a loving parent:
    - "It's okay to say what you need."
    - "You're not being mean. You're being real."
    - "Your feelings matter too."

Use the "Truth Sandwich" Technique

- A loving way to be honest:
  - Start with kindness or appreciation.
  - Share your truth clearly.
  - End with empathy or care.
    - Example: "I care about you and I want to be honest. I felt overwhelmed by the way things happened yesterday. I know we can work through it together".

Tune Into Your Body's Truth

- When you're unsure whether to speak up, ask:
  - What's happening in my body right now?
  - Do I feel tight, tense, or anxious? Am I shrinking?
- Your body often knows the truth before your mind does.

Watch + Learn from Graceful Truth-Tellers

- Observe people (real or fictional) who speak truth with kindness.
  - What tone do they use?
  - How do they hold compassion and honesty together?
- Role models expand what feels possible.

Celebrate Every Time You Speak Up

- No matter how small:
  - "I shared how I felt. I'm proud of that."
  - "I asked for what I needed. That's brave."
- This rewires your brain to see assertiveness as safe and rewarding.

Speaking your truth with love is both courageous and kind, to yourself and to others.

Assertiveness is not harsh or selfish; it is a way to honor your needs while showing respect for those around you. Each small moment you choose honesty over silence, clarity over fear, builds confidence, strengthens your voice, and deepens connection.

Remember, you don't need to speak loudly to be heard. You don't need to sacrifice your peace to be kind.

By redefining assertiveness as love, every gentle "no," every honest expression, becomes a bridge to greater self-respect, safer relationships, and a life where your voice matters.

Journal Prompt: What does it mean to honor yourself and others at the same time?

Redefine Assertiveness as Love

Personal Notes / Journaling

Redefine Assertiveness as Love

Personal Notes / Journaling

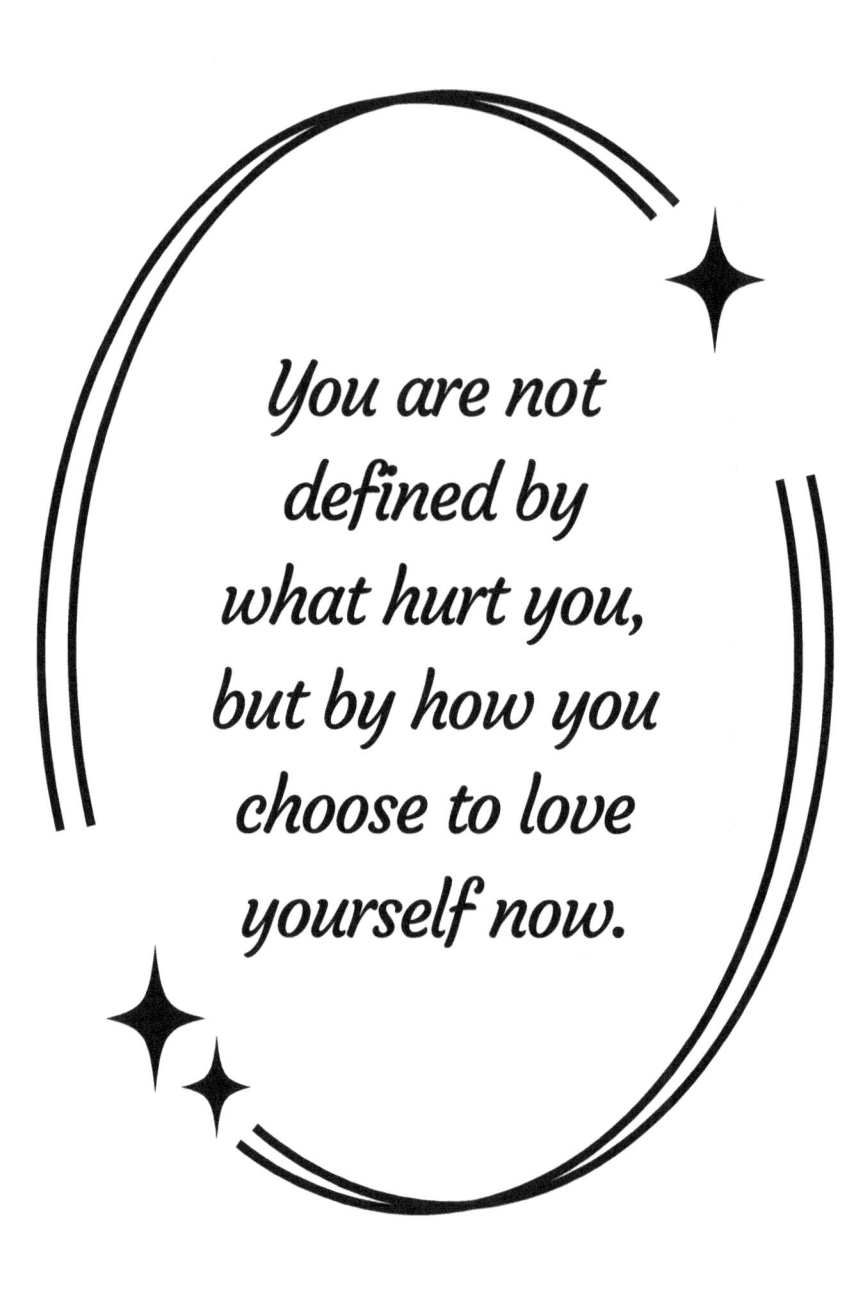

STEP SEVEN

Heal the Root Wounds

Purpose: Gently tend to the original pain.

Many patterns come from old wounds, the moments you felt invisible, rejected, or silenced. Give your younger self the love and validation she needed. You are your own healer now.

Try inner child journaling, meditations, or simply speaking gently to yourself when you're triggered.

MANTRA

I release the past.
I forgive and grow.

Visualize your younger self and send her compassion and light.

Repeat this daily.

Healing Core Wounds

Healing root wounds is sacred, tender work.

This step will help you not only understand why you feel unworthy, silenced, or small, but actually begin to unravel and transform those painful origins with love and compassion.

The hardest part for me was looking back with honesty. Not just remembering what happened, but feeling it. Letting myself truly witness the moments I had buried for so long:

The nights I cried myself to sleep, silently praying for something to change. The days I walked on eggshells, convincing myself, "Maybe this is just how love is". And the quiet moments when I thought, "Maybe this is all I deserve".

There was a time I didn't think I could survive those memories. But what I discovered is this:

Healing isn't about erasing the past. It's about holding your younger self with love and saying, "You didn't deserve that, and it wasn't your fault."

I began writing letters to her, to the girl I used to be. Letters that said:

"You are not too much."
"You are worthy of love."
"You are not broken. You are becoming."
"God doesn't make mistakes."
"You were made to stand out, to be your own person."

Some days, it felt like my heart would break all over again. But as I returned to those wounds with compassion instead of shame, something began to shift.

I realized I wasn't broken. I was healing. I wasn't weak. I was brave. And the parts of me I used to hide became the very parts that made me powerful.

Healing the root wounds didn't erase the pain, but it helped me rise above it. It helped me become the woman I was always meant to be.

Here's an expanded guide with powerful practices and approaches to help you gently heal your core wounds and reclaim your voice.

Inner Child Healing Practices

So many wounds begin in childhood: times we felt unseen, unsafe, or unworthy. Healing the inner child is about giving her the love and safety she never received. Practices:

- Write to her regularly: "Little me, I see you. I'm so sorry you felt… I will protect you now."
- Speak aloud to a photo of your younger self.
- Hold a stuffed animal, pillow, or your own hand to comfort the "little you."
- Meditate or visualize your younger self in a safe place, receiving hugs, affirmation, and love.

Guided Inner Child Meditations

Take time to listen to guided meditations that walk you through:

- Meeting your younger self.
- Offering safety and validation.
- Rewriting the memory with comfort and love.

Try this simple visualization:

Close your eyes. Picture your younger self in a place that feels safe. Walk toward her. Kneel down. Tell her: "You didn't deserve that. It wasn't your fault. You are so loved."

Name the Wound Without Shame

Gently invite reflection on:

- What beliefs were born from that wound? (e.g., "I'm not enough," "My feelings are too much," "If I speak up, I'll be abandoned")
- Whose voice or action caused this belief to form?
- Is that belief still true today, or was it never true to begin with?

Letting the truth rise is a form of healing in itself.

Nurturing Moments

Nurturing is showing up for yourself in the way your caregivers couldn't.

- Ask yourself: "What do I need right now?" and honor it.
- Offer a self-soothing touch: hand on your heart, gentle rocking, warm baths, cozy blankets.
- Giving yourself permission to rest, cry, say no, or take up space.

Art & Symbolic Healing

Some women find healing through creativity, especially if speaking is hard.

- Draw or paint your inner child or a symbolic image of your healing journey.
- Create a "Healing Box" filled with comforting items for emotional regulation.
- Write poems or songs to your younger self.

Memory Rewrite Page

- Recall a painful memory.
- Visualize a new outcome.
- Write what you wish had happened.

Forgiveness (With Boundaries)

Clarify that forgiveness doesn't mean excusing harm. It means releasing yourself from the grip of the past.

- Write a forgiveness letter you never send.
- Say aloud: "I choose peace over resentment. I release this to free myself."
- Visualize cutting cords or releasing old pain into the earth or light.

Root Belief Excavation

- What is an old belief holding you back?
- Where did it start?
- How did it make you feel?
- Replace that old truth with a new truth to believe now.

Daily Affirmations for the Wounded Self

Repeat gentle truths like:

- "I am not broken. I am healing."
- "I am allowed to feel and still be safe."
- "That was then. This is now. I am safe and loved."

Say them while looking into a mirror, while holding your heart, or while journaling.

Safe Release Practices

Wounds store energy in the body. Gently releasing emotions is crucial.

- Cry in a safe space without judgment.
- Shake or dance to release pent-up fear or pain.
- Journal unfiltered anger or grief and then tear up the paper.

Healing your root wounds is gentle, sacred work. It is not about erasing the past, but about holding your younger self with love and compassion.

Each time you witness, validate, and comfort the little you, you release shame, reclaim your power, and step closer to your true voice.

This work takes courage, patience, and tenderness, but every act of care, like writing a letter, speaking kindly to yourself, or simply being present with your pain, is a step toward wholeness. By tending to these original hurts, you are not only healing old wounds, you are creating space to live freely, authentically, and fully.

You are your own healer. You are safe. You are worthy. And this love you give yourself will ripple into every part of your life.

Journal Prompt: What parts of yourself did you hide to feel safe or accepted? How can you begin to honor and express those parts today?

Heal the Root Wounds

Personal Notes / Journaling

STEP EIGHT

Celebrate Progress and Small Wins

Purpose: Reinforce growth and build confidence.

Every step you take is worth celebrating.

Notice and honor your growth.

Whether it's a whispered "no" or a bold choice, you're showing up for yourself. That's powerful.

MANTRA

Every small step is a victory.
I am proud of me.

Smile and feel gratitude for how far you've come.

Repeat this daily.

Ways to Celebrate Progress and Small Wins

Celebrating small wins is an essential step.

It helps retrain your brain to recognize your worth, reinforce self-belief, and create positive momentum.

For so long, I believed progress had to look big to matter. I thought healing meant breakthroughs, bold steps, and life-changing moments.

So I overlooked the quiet victories. The mornings I got out of bed when it was hard, the deep breaths I took instead of breaking down, the times I said no when I would've said yes just to keep the peace.

But in the hardest season of my life, after the medical incident, when I was learning to walk again, healing the wounds on my leg, running my business from a recliner, and fighting to stay hopeful, I realized something profound. Every small step is a miracle.

The first time I stood up without help. The first time I laughed again. The first time I ate solid food without feeling sick. The first time I opened my laptop and kept going, even when it felt impossible.

These weren't little things. They were proof. Proof that I was healing. Proof that I was stronger than I thought. Proof that I was rewriting my story in real time.

So now, I am grateful, and I celebrate it all. The whispered prayers. The tiny wins. The messy progress. Because every step forward, no matter how small, is sacred.

I've learned to ask myself, "What can I celebrate today?" Sometimes, the answer is simply, "I didn't give up." And that is more than enough.

There are some practical, joyful, and meaningful ways you can celebrate your progress.

Create a "Victory Jar" or "Proud-of-Me Box"

- Write each small win on a slip of paper and place it in a jar or decorative box.
- Read them on tough days to remember how far you've come.
- Add stickers, symbols, or affirmations to make it feel magical and personal.

Keep a "Confidence Journal"

- Dedicate one notebook or section of a journal to tracking wins, growth, and moments of bravery.
- Use prompts like: "Today I honored myself by…," or "One thing I did that felt empowering…"

Use Movement as Celebration

- Do a little happy dance after doing something hard.
- Take a joyful walk and reflect on your growth.
- Play your favorite song and move in a way that feels free and proud.

Use Visual Trackers

- Draw a path, flower petals, or staircase, and color in a part every time you grow or choose yourself.
- Use stickers, stamps, or washi tape in your journal to mark wins.

Reward Yourself with Simple Pleasures

- Choose small, meaningful treats:
    - A new journal or pen
    - A solo coffee date
    - A fresh bouquet of flowers
    - 30 minutes of uninterrupted "me time"

These don't have to be expensive, just intentional.

Voice Notes to Self

- Record short voice memos saying, "I did something brave today," or "I'm proud of myself because…"
- Listen back when self-doubt creeps in.

Create a Personal Ritual

- Mark progress with intention and self-love.
    - Light a candle for every courageous choice.
    - Take a warm bath with essential oils after a challenging boundary was set.
    - Toast yourself with a mug of tea or sparkling water.

Tell a Trusted Friend or Supportive Group

- Share your wins with someone who truly sees and celebrates you.
- Text a best friend, post in a healing circle, or write a letter to someone who would be proud of you.

Affirm Your Progress Out Loud

- Look in the mirror and say:
    - "I'm proud of how I showed up today."
    - "That took courage, and I did it."
    - "I am becoming the woman I dreamed of being."

Every step you take, no matter how small, is worthy of recognition. Celebrating these moments reminds you that healing, growth, and transformation are happening, even when it feels quiet or slow.

Each choice to show up for yourself, each gentle boundary, each act of courage, is proof of your strength and resilience. By honoring these small wins, you reinforce your worth, build confidence, and create momentum toward the life you are reclaiming.

Remember, progress doesn't have to be dramatic to be meaningful. Every step forward is important. Every whisper of "I tried" matters.

And by celebrating these victories, you give yourself permission to see how far you've truly come.

Journal Prompt: What small win are you celebrating this week?

Celebrate Progress and Small Wins

Personal Notes / Journaling

Celebrate Progress and Small Wins

Personal Notes / Journaling

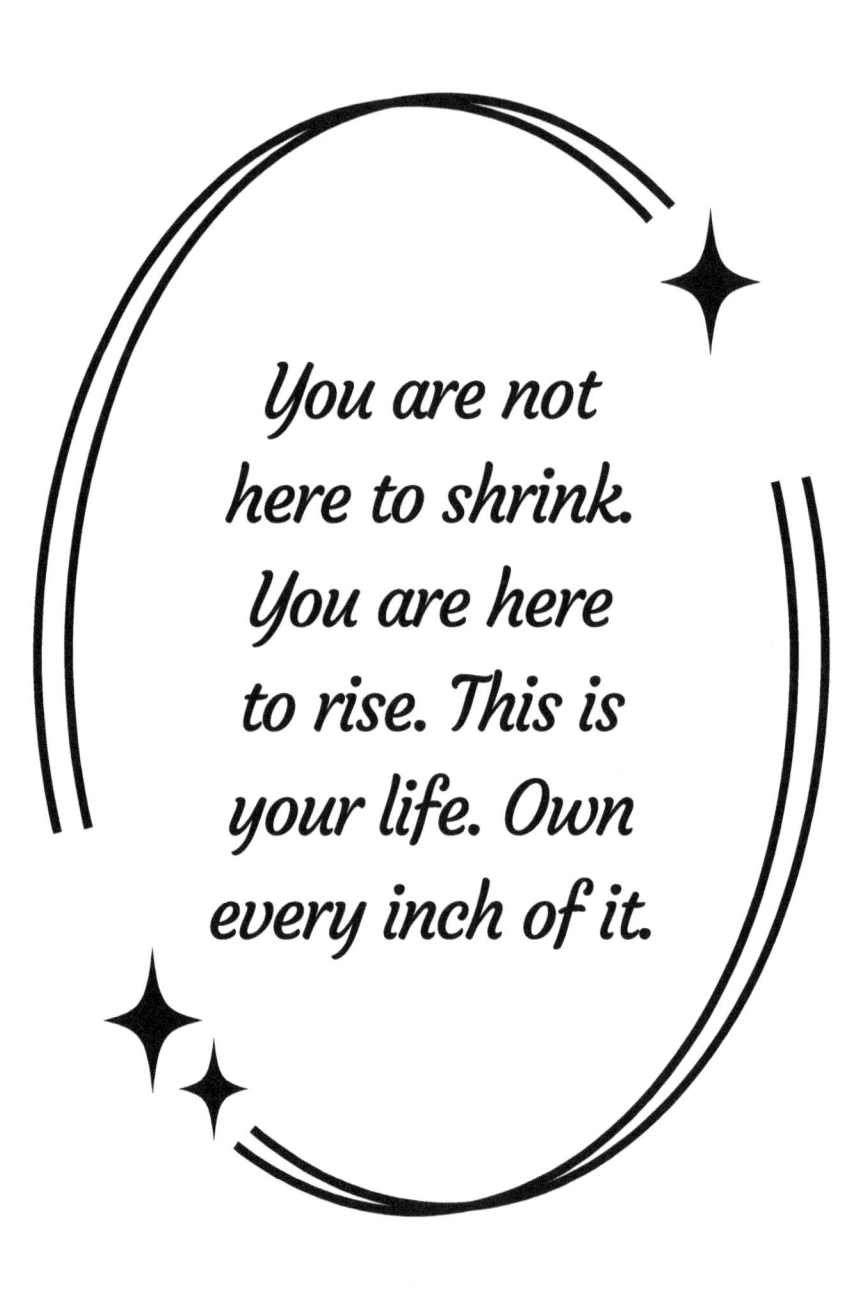

You are not here to shrink. You are here to rise. This is your life. Own every inch of it.

STEP NINE

Take Ownership of Your Life

Purpose: Step into your power and write your next chapter.

You don't need permission to live the life you want.

This is your story, and you get to choose what happens next.

Step boldly into your power. Make decisions that align with your values and dreams.

MANTRA

This is my life.
I choose boldly, love deeply, and rise daily.

Breathe in courage. Exhale doubt. Stand tall in your power.

Repeat this daily.

Take Ownership and Step Into Your Power

This step is where the transformation becomes embodied.

Taking ownership is about living with intention, acting from self-worth, and no longer waiting for outside validation.

When I almost died, everything changed. Lying in that hospital bed, with no feeling in my leg, unable to walk, and unsure if I'd ever walk again, I had one overwhelming thought. I haven't done what I came here to do.

I hadn't written the books. I hadn't shared my message. I hadn't fully lived my life, only the version of it shaped by fear, people-pleasing, and survival.

In that stillness, between life and loss, I heard my inner voice louder than ever before. It didn't whisper. It roared.

This is your story. Stop waiting for someone else to write it.

I realized I had been waiting. Waiting for the "right" time. Waiting for someone to give me permission. Waiting to feel ready, confident, or perfect. But waiting never gave me the life I wanted. Choosing did.

Five months after that incident, after nearly losing my life, I published my first book.

Not because I was fully healed or had it all figured out. Because I decided to not waste my second chance and finally take ownership. To choose now. To move forward imperfectly. To say, "This is my one life, and I won't waste another moment sitting on the sidelines of it."

Taking ownership isn't about having all the answers. It's about making one powerful decision after another. To believe in yourself. To pursue your passion. To live boldly, deeply, and on purpose.

You don't need permission to write a new chapter. You just need to pick up the pen.

Here are some powerful and practical ways you can fully step into your power and take ownership of your life.

Declare Your Personal Values

- Write down 3–5 core values that define what matters most to you.
- Use them as a compass for decisions: "Does this choice honor my values?"
- This helps you lead your life instead of reacting to it.

Create a Vision Board or Life Map

- Collect images, words, and affirmations that represent your ideal life.
- Don't hold back. Dream boldly and create a vision that excites you.
- Look at it regularly to stay connected to your goals and desires.

Practice Saying "I Choose" Instead of "I Have To"

- Swap disempowering language for ownership:
  - Instead of "I have to go to work," say "I choose to work because I value financial freedom."
  - Instead of "I can't say no," say "I choose to honor my energy."

Take Intentional, Imperfect Action

- Power comes from doing, not waiting until things are perfect.
- Choose one uncomfortable but meaningful action each week (speaking up, applying for something, making a change).
- Celebrate your courage, not just your outcome.

Live by Your Own Definitions of Success and Happiness

- Define what success and happiness mean to you, not society, family, or culture.
- Ask: "What would a fulfilled life look and feel like to ME?"
- Write your answers and let them guide your daily actions.

Set "Non-Negotiables" for Your Life

- Let go of relationships that dim your light or disrespect your boundaries, and spend more time with those who uplift, inspire, and mirror your growth.
- What are 3–5 things you will no longer compromise on? (Respect, rest, boundaries, creativity, peace, etc.)
- Revisit them often and use them to guide relationships, work, and choices.

Write a New "Life Mission" Statement

- Example: "I am a woman who leads with love, speaks with strength, and walks in purpose."
- Write it in bold letters. Say it out loud every morning.

Own Your Story Without Shame

- Journal or speak your story from a place of strength, not victimhood.
- Use empowering phrases like:
  - "I survived and I've grown stronger."
  - "I'm not broken. I'm becoming."

Practice Daily Power Rituals

- Start your day with affirmations, breathwork, or visualization.
- End your day by asking: "Did I live from my truth today?" If not, what can shift tomorrow?
- Power is a daily choice, not a destination.

Taking ownership of your life is an invitation to step fully into your power. You don't need permission, validation, or perfect timing. Your story belongs to you, and every choice you make shapes the next chapter.

Each intentional decision, each imperfect step forward, is proof that you are reclaiming your voice, your dreams, and your life.

Ownership is not about having all the answers; it's about showing up for yourself, trusting your inner compass, and moving forward with courage.

When you choose to live boldly, to define your own success, and to honor your values, you write a story that reflects your true self.

This is your life. Own it. Live it. Celebrate it.

Journal Prompt: Declare one bold, empowering action you'll take this week.

Take Ownership of Your Life

Personal Notes / Journaling

Take Ownership of Your Life

Personal Notes / Journaling

The stories you tell yourself shape the life you live. You have the power to rewrite them.

STEP TEN

Rewrite Your Self Story

Purpose: Shift from powerlessness to empowerment.

You are not who you used to be. You are becoming someone strong, resilient, and worthy.

Start crafting a new narrative. Instead of, "I'm too sensitive," try, "My sensitivity is a strength."

You are the author of your life. What kind of story do you want to write?

MANTRA

I am not who I was.
I am who I choose to become.

Close your eyes and see yourself walking boldly into your new story.

Repeat this daily.

Rewriting Your Story

Rewriting your self story is one of the most transformative steps of the healing journey.

It's how you move from old, limiting narratives rooted in pain, trauma, or survival into new, empowered identities rooted in truth, choice, and self-worth.

When I was young, people said I was brave. Smart. Creative. Confident. I believed them, for a while.

But then life happened. I faced years of bullying that made me question my worth. I entered a marriage where my voice was gradually silenced. The strong, vibrant girl I once was slowly disappeared beneath layers of fear, doubt, anxiety, and survival.

I began to believe a different story, one where I was too sensitive, paranoid, too emotional, and not good enough. A story where my dreams didn't matter, and my needs came last.

So I stayed small. I stayed quiet. I thought disappearing would keep me safe. But here's what I learned. Hiding doesn't protect you. It just disconnects you from the life you're meant to live.

Rewriting my story meant looking those old beliefs in the face and saying, "That's not who I am anymore." It meant letting go of shame for the things I tolerated. It meant honoring the girl who did the best she could with what she had. And it meant choosing a new narrative. One written in my own words, with truth and intention.

Now, I don't just hope for a better story. I write it.

Every boundary I set. Every dream I chase. Every time I speak up. I'm turning the page.

Because I am not who I was. I am who I choose to become.

Here are some powerful practices and exercises to help you rewrite your story with intention, love, and clarity.

Identify the Old Narrative First

- "What beliefs have I carried about myself that are no longer true?"
- "Where did this story come from? Was it someone else's voice?"
- Awareness is the first step to reclaiming authorship.

Create a New Identity Statement

- "I am a woman who..."
  - "...knows her value."
  - "...shows up fully."
  - "...leads with compassion and strength."

These become truth anchors to return to daily.

Write a Personal Empowerment Manifesto

- A short paragraph declaring:
  - Who you are now.
  - What you believe.
  - What you're no longer available for.
  - What you are calling in.

Example: "I no longer shrink to fit in. I speak with strength and live with open-hearted courage. I am no longer apologizing for who I am becoming."

Reframe Limiting Labels into Strengths

- Turn old labels on their head:
  - "Too emotional" → "Deeply intuitive and compassionate"
  - "Too quiet" → "Thoughtful and wise"
  - "Too sensitive" → "Empathetic and attuned to others

Use Story Language to Take Ownership

- Write your story like a heroine's journey:
    - "I once believed __, but now I know __."
    - "The moment I chose myself was when __."
    - "What tried to break me taught me how to __."

Create a "Story Shift" Vision Board

- Include images, affirmations, and keywords that represent:
    - Who you are becoming.
    - How you want to feel.
    - The life you are now choosing.

Daily "I Am Becoming" Journal Practice

- Each day, finish this sentence:
    - "I am becoming a woman who…"
- This keeps the new identity alive and evolving.

Speak the New Story Out Loud

- Speaking is powerful for integration.
- Practice saying:
    - "This is who I used to be… but here's who I am now."
    - "I am proud of the woman I'm becoming."
    - "My story is one of rising."

Rewriting your self story is not about denying your past. It's about honoring it without letting it define you. Every chapter you've lived, every wound you've healed, and every truth you've reclaimed has brought you here to this moment of choice.

You are no longer living from survival, silence, or old scripts written by fear or circumstance. You are stepping into authorship.

With each new belief you choose, each loving boundary you set, and each truth you speak, you are writing a story rooted in worth, courage, and intention.

Your story is not finished. It is unfolding. And from here forward, the words belong to you.

You are the author.

You hold the pen.

And you can write the next chapter with hope, power, and purpose.

Journal Prompt: Turn your transformation into a 1-page empowered story "script" you can read when you need strength.

Rewrite Your Self-Story

Personal Notes / Journaling

Rewrite Your Self-Story

Personal Notes / Journaling

CONCLUSION

This Is Just the Beginning

You've just walked through a powerful 10-step journey. One that led you back to your voice, your truth, your worth.

You've done the brave work of uncovering old beliefs, setting new boundaries, speaking up with love, and reclaiming your story.

You've begun to heal wounds that once silenced you.

You've practiced self-compassion, stood up for your needs, and taken ownership of your life.

That's not small. That's revolutionary.

And while this chapter of the journey is complete, your story is still being written, one empowered choice at a time.

You don't have to have it all figured out.

You only need to keep showing up for yourself with truth and love. Again and again.

If you're ready to go deeper, to continue your healing and transformation with guidance and support, I'd love to walk alongside you.

Visit my site for more information about how I help women fully step into their voice, power, and purpose, become the heroine of their story, and write life story movies that leave a legacy. And **download a FREE copy** of the "Finding Your Voice" workbook for more journal prompts and pages.

Link: anncknickell.com

Write your own story, one empowered choice at a time.

www.ingramcontent.com/pod-product-compliance
Lightning Source LLC
Chambersburg PA
CBHW070627050426
42450CB00011B/3138